Strategic Power

8 Principles for Leading with Vision and Impact

Elianna Sage

Copyright © 2024 Elianna Sage

All rights reserved. No part of this book may be reproduced or transmitted in any form or by any means, electronic or mechanical, including photocopying, recording, or by any information storage and retrieval system, without written permission from the author.

This book is a work of nonfiction. The views expressed are solely those of the author and do not necessarily reflect the views of the publisher, who hereby disclaims any responsibility for them.

Acknowledgements

Writing this book has been an incredible journey, and it wouldn't have been possible without the support and encouragement of so many people. I'd like to take a moment to express my deepest gratitude to those who have been a part of this process.

First and foremost, I want to thank my family. To my partner, whose unwavering belief in me kept me going through long nights and countless revisions—you are my foundation, and I am eternally grateful for your love, patience, and encouragement. To my children, who inspire me daily with their curiosity, joy, and endless energy—you remind me of the importance of balance and living with purpose.

To my mentors and colleagues who have guided me over the years: your wisdom, support, and feedback have been invaluable. You've not only helped shape my thinking on leadership but also challenged me to grow, both personally and professionally. I'm especially grateful to those who've shared their stories and experiences with me, helping to broaden my perspective and deepen my understanding of what it means to lead with integrity and purpose.

To my friends who have been my sounding board throughout this process—thank you for your insight, for listening to my ideas (and frustrations), and for always encouraging me to keep pushing forward. Your belief in this project has been a source of motivation and strength.

I'd also like to express my appreciation to the incredible team who helped bring this book to life. To my editor, whose keen eye and thoughtful suggestions helped polish this work into what it is today—your attention to detail and understanding of my vision were truly a gift. To the entire publishing team, thank you for your expertise, guidance, and dedication to making this project a success.

Finally, to the readers—this book is for you. Whether you are just starting your leadership journey or are well into it, I hope the lessons and stories shared here serve as a source of inspiration, practical guidance, and encouragement. Thank you for trusting me with your time and attention. It is my hope that this book not only helps you achieve your goals but also empowers you to make a lasting impact on those around you.

With heartfelt thanks,

Elianna Sage

Dedication

To my family—my greatest source of strength and inspiration.

To my partner, for your endless love, support, and belief in me. To my children, who remind me every day of the importance of leading with both heart and purpose.

And to every aspiring leader who dares to dream big and make a lasting impact—this book is for you.

Table of Contents page

Introduction to Strategic Power: 8 Principles for Leading with Vision and Impact 9

    Why Vision Matters 10

    Leading with Impact..12

    The Power of Principles 13

    Connecting to Your Core Values 15

    Your Journey Starts Now 16

Chapter 1: The Power of Vision 18

    1.1 Understanding the Role of Vision in Leadership..............18

    1.2 Crafting Your Vision 21

    1.3 Communicating Your Vision Effectively 25

Chapter 2: Principled Leadership...29

    2.1 What It Means to Lead with Principles 29

    2.2 Identifying and Committing to Your Core Principles........33

    2.3 Embodying Your Principles as a Leader 36

Chapter 3: Building a Strategic Mindset 40

    3.1 Shifting from Reactive to Proactive Leadership...............41

    3.2 Setting Clear, Long-Term Objectives...............................44

    3.3 Staying Agile in a Changing Environment 47

Chapter 4: Emotional Intelligence in Leadership 51

    4.1 The Foundation of Emotional Intelligence (EQ)...............52

    4.2 Developing Your EQ as a Leader 57

    4.3 Leveraging EQ for Team Success.....................................60

Chapter 5: Influence and Persuasion: The Art of Guiding Others 64

   5.1 Understanding Influence vs. Authority 65

   5.2 Mastering Persuasion Techniques 69

   5.3 Expanding Your Sphere of Influence 73

Chapter 6: Building High-Performing Teams 79

Introduction to Strategic Power: 8 Principles for Leading with Vision and Impact

When I think about the word "leadership," I don't just picture someone standing at the front of a room, speaking to a crowd, or commanding a team. Leadership, in its truest form, is about more than just position or power. It's about guiding with purpose, leading with vision, and creating a lasting impact in the lives of others. I believe that deep down, you want to do more than just succeed. You want to lead with integrity, transform the world around you, and leave a legacy that matters.

Maybe you've always known you had the potential to lead, but something has held you back. Or perhaps you're already in a leadership position but feel like you're just scratching the surface of what's possible. You might be navigating challenges, feeling overwhelmed by the demands of leadership, or questioning if you're on the right path. Wherever you are on your journey, I want you to know that leadership is not just a title or a role. It's a calling. And it's one that, with the right guidance, you can answer with confidence, clarity, and conviction.

This book, *Strategic Power: 8 Principles for Leading with Vision and Impact*, is about unlocking that potential within you. It's about giving you the tools, strategies, and mindset shifts needed to lead with strength and purpose. Whether you're leading a small team, a growing company, or simply striving to lead yourself more effectively, these principles are designed to resonate with your core values and aspirations. My goal is to help you step into your full power and become the kind of leader who not only achieves great things but does so in a way that inspires and uplifts those around you.

Why Vision Matters

In my experience, one of the most powerful attributes of a great leader is their ability to cast a compelling vision. A vision is more than just a goal or an objective. It's the story you tell yourself and others about the future you're working to create. A strong vision is magnetic—it draws people in, gives them a sense of purpose, and inspires them to strive for something bigger than themselves. When you lead with vision, you're not just managing tasks or chasing after short-term wins. You're leading people toward a future they believe in, one that aligns with their deepest values and dreams.

But here's the thing: having a vision isn't enough. You have to know how to communicate it in a way that resonates with others. You have to make people see and feel that vision in their bones. And most importantly, you have to live that vision every single day, through your actions, decisions, and presence. Leading with vision requires courage, because sometimes the path forward isn't clear, and other times, it may feel like no one else sees the possibilities you see. But it's your ability to hold that vision steadfastly, even in the face of challenges, that will set you apart as a leader.

Ask yourself: What kind of future do you want to create? What does success look like to you, not just in terms of material achievements, but in terms of the impact you have on the people and the world around you? If you're reading this book, it's because you want to lead with purpose, and that purpose starts with your vision.

Leading with Impact

Vision without impact is just a dream. To truly lead, you need to turn that vision into tangible results—results that not only drive your personal and professional success but also create meaningful change for others. That's what I mean by impact. Impact is about more than hitting targets or climbing the corporate ladder. It's about leaving a lasting imprint on the lives you touch, the teams you lead, and the communities you serve.

Think about the leaders who have inspired you. The ones who made a difference in your life, not just because they were good at what they did, but because they made you feel seen, valued, and empowered. That's the kind of leader you have the potential to be. A leader who, through their vision and actions, elevates those around them. When you focus on leading with impact, you move from a mindset of self-centered achievement to one of service and contribution.

The world needs leaders like you—leaders who are not only driven to succeed but who are committed to making a difference. Whether it's through innovation, mentorship, or social change, your ability to make an impact is what will define your legacy as a leader. And the truth is, the greater your impact, the more fulfilling your journey will be. This book will guide you through the principles that will help you maximize your impact and leave a legacy that endures.

The Power of Principles

In *Strategic Power*, we'll be exploring eight core principles that form the foundation of effective leadership. These principles are not abstract theories or lofty ideals. They are practical, actionable strategies that will empower you to lead with vision and impact. Each principle is designed to tap into your inner strengths, challenge you to grow, and equip you with the tools needed to navigate the complexities of leadership in today's world.

But before we dive into those principles, I want to emphasize something important: leadership is a journey, not a destination. There is no "one-size-fits-all" formula for success. The principles I'm about to share with you are meant to serve as a guide, but how you apply them will be unique to you. It will depend on your circumstances, your values, and your goals. My role is to help you discover the leader within and provide you with the insights and strategies that will allow you to lead authentically and powerfully.

Throughout this book, I'll encourage you to reflect deeply on what kind of leader you want to be. Not just in terms of your skills or achievements, but in terms of your character, your integrity, and your purpose. True leadership is about more than just getting people to follow you—it's about creating a vision so compelling, and an impact so meaningful, that people are inspired to join you on your journey.

Connecting to Your Core Values

One of the most powerful ways to lead with vision and impact is by aligning your leadership with your core values. Your values are the beliefs and principles that define who you are at your core. They are the compass that guides your decisions, your actions, and your interactions with others. When you lead from a place of authenticity, grounded in your values, you naturally inspire trust and loyalty. People are drawn to leaders who are real, who stand for something, and who live their values in everything they do.

But living and leading from your values isn't always easy. It requires self-awareness, discipline, and sometimes, the courage to stand alone in your convictions. In a world that often prioritizes short-term gains over long-term impact, it can be tempting to compromise on your values for the sake of convenience or expediency. But I'm here to remind you that real leadership isn't about taking the easy path—it's about choosing the right path, even when it's hard.

So take a moment to reflect on your values. What matters most to you? What are the non-negotiables in your life and leadership? The more clarity you have around your values, the more aligned your vision and impact will be. And when you lead from this place of alignment, you'll not only feel more fulfilled and confident, but you'll also inspire others to do the same.

Your Journey Starts Now

As you embark on this journey through *Strategic Power*, I want you to know that you already have everything you need within you to become the leader you aspire to be. The principles I'll be sharing with you are meant to unlock and amplify the strengths that are already inside you. Whether you're stepping into leadership for the first time or seeking to deepen your impact as an experienced leader, this book is your roadmap to success.

The journey of leadership is one of continuous growth, learning, and transformation. It's about pushing past your comfort zones, embracing new challenges, and constantly striving to become the best version of yourself. I'm honored to be a part of your journey and to walk alongside you as you step into your full power as a leader.

The time is now. You've been called to lead, to make a difference, and to create a legacy that matters. The question is: are you ready to answer that call?

Let's begin.

Chapter 1: The Power of Vision

1.1 Understanding the Role of Vision in Leadership

When I first stepped into a leadership role, I thought the key to success was setting clear goals and working hard to achieve them. But as I learned the hard way, this approach was missing something crucial. I didn't have a unifying vision—a bigger picture that tied everything together. I was too focused on day-to-day operations, on checking boxes and meeting deadlines, and my team mirrored that lack of direction. Without a vision, we were just moving aimlessly. This was my first lesson in understanding the profound role vision plays in leadership.

1.1.1 Defining Vision in Leadership

Vision in leadership is more than just a lofty ideal or a "mission statement" on a wall. It's about creating a vivid picture of the future that pulls you and your team forward. It provides a sense of purpose, not only for you as a leader but for every individual who contributes to making that vision a reality. Vision shapes not just what you do, but how and why you do it. It gives your team a reason to care and connects them emotionally to the work. A true leader uses vision to inspire, motivate, and focus their team's energy on something greater than individual tasks.

1.1.2 Vision vs. Goals

I remember being caught up in the whirlwind of meeting specific goals and targets early in my career. Goals are essential, but they are not the end game. It wasn't until I realized the difference between vision and goals that I could lead effectively. Goals are the milestones along the way; vision is the final destination. It's the guiding light that helps you determine which goals matter most and ensures that your daily actions align with long-term aspirations.

Think of vision as the compass that gives you direction, while goals are the steps that help you navigate toward that destination. Without vision, goals can feel empty—like running a race without knowing why you're doing it. But when every goal supports a compelling vision, it creates a sense of purpose and cohesion.

1.1.3 The Emotional and Strategic Importance of Vision

Vision not only serves as a strategic roadmap but also connects with people on a deeper, emotional level. As humans, we're motivated by meaning. We want to feel that the work we do matters and that we're part of something bigger than ourselves. A compelling vision taps into that need, providing a sense of purpose that energizes people, even in challenging times. When I finally articulated a clear and meaningful vision for my team, their engagement skyrocketed. Suddenly, they weren't just working for a paycheck—they were contributing to something important, something they believed in.

Emotional Intelligence and Vision

To effectively convey this kind of vision, emotional intelligence (EQ) is critical. Emotional intelligence allows you to understand and manage your own emotions and those of your team. A leader with high EQ can tap into the emotional undercurrents within the team, understand their needs, and connect the vision to those emotional drivers. This creates a sense of shared purpose and fosters loyalty. Leaders who are emotionally intelligent are more adept at anticipating emotional responses, guiding team members through periods of uncertainty, and maintaining high levels of motivation.

For example, when launching a new initiative, I've seen emotionally intelligent leaders use vision not just to describe what success looks like but to validate the emotions of their team—acknowledging fears, concerns, or excitement. They know that people need to feel seen and heard before they can fully commit to a new direction.

1.2 Crafting Your Vision

Crafting a vision is not a one-time exercise. It's a process that requires deep introspection and understanding of your core values and purpose, as well as a reflection on your personal journey.

1.2.1 Identifying Your Core Values and Purpose

Your vision begins with your values—those fundamental beliefs that guide your actions. For me, it took time to identify what truly mattered. After some reflection, I realized that empowerment, integrity, and innovation were central to who I was as a leader. These values weren't just personal preferences—they were the principles that informed every decision I made, from hiring team members to setting long-term strategies.

Case Study; Nelson Mandela

Take Nelson Mandela, for example. His vision for a unified, democratic South Africa was deeply rooted in his core values of equality and justice. Even during his 27 years of imprisonment, he never wavered in his vision. He embodied the emotional intelligence necessary to understand the needs and fears of the people he aimed to lead, and his deep commitment to his values gave his vision credibility.

For you, identifying your core values is essential to crafting an authentic vision. Without this grounding, your vision risks being just a set of empty words. Ask yourself: what do I stand for? What values do I want to embody in my leadership? The answers to these questions will shape the foundation of your vision.

1.2.2 Reflecting on Your Past, Present, and Future

Your vision is also shaped by your experiences—both the successes and the setbacks. Reflecting on my past helped me see the patterns in my leadership journey, the lessons I'd learned, and the aspirations I had for the future. Taking stock of your personal journey helps you create a vision that is not only aspirational but also deeply meaningful.

Consider how your past informs your vision. What lessons have you learned along the way? What challenges have shaped your perspective? Reflecting on these experiences can help you clarify where you want to go and how you plan to get there.

Case Study: Howard Schultz

Howard Schultz, the former CEO of Starbucks, used his personal experiences growing up in a poor family to shape his vision for the company. He wanted to create a company that not only provided a great product but also treated its employees (whom he called "partners") with dignity and respect. His vision wasn't just about selling coffee—it was about creating a company culture that reflected his values of community and equality.

1.2.3 Creating a Vision Statement

Once you've identified your core values and reflected on your journey, it's time to craft a clear and compelling vision statement. This isn't just a tagline—it's the North Star that will guide you and your team.

Your vision statement should be concise, clear, and inspiring. It should answer three essential questions:

1. What future state do you want to achieve?
2. Why does it matter?
3. How will you get there?

Potential Challenges:

Crafting a vision can feel daunting. One challenge I've seen leaders face is the pressure to come up with something "perfect" right away. The truth is, your vision will evolve over time as you and your team grow. Start with what feels right, and allow your vision to adapt as you gain more clarity. Also, resist the temptation to make your vision too broad or vague. A vision that's too lofty can feel disconnected from reality and hard to execute. Focus on something tangible and meaningful that people can rally behind.

1.3 Communicating Your Vision Effectively

Having a clear vision is only the first step. If you can't communicate it effectively, it won't inspire or mobilize your team. This was another critical lesson for me as a leader. Early on, I struggled to get buy-in because I wasn't communicating my vision in a way that resonated with others.

1.3.1 The Power of Storytelling in Leadership

I learned the power of storytelling when I first tried to explain my vision to my team. At first, I used logical arguments and data to show why our new direction made sense. But it didn't click with them until I shared a personal story—one that connected emotionally with their own experiences.

Emotional Intelligence in Storytelling

As leaders, we need to connect emotionally with our audience. When you tell stories, make sure they tap into shared values and experiences. Emotional intelligence helps you gauge how your story will resonate with different people. The stories you choose should reflect the emotions and aspirations of your team, making them feel like they're part of the journey.

1.3.2 Tailoring Your Vision for Different Audiences

Different audiences have different needs and perspectives. I learned this when I first communicated my vision to upper management, and then separately to my team. The management team wanted to know how the vision would impact the bottom line. My team, on the other hand, cared about how the vision aligned with their personal goals and work-life balance.

Tailor your vision communication to address the concerns and aspirations of each audience. For example, stakeholders might need to see a clear ROI, while your team might want to understand how the vision connects to their career development or personal growth.

1.3.3 Living Your Vision

Finally, your actions speak louder than your words. Living your vision means aligning your daily decisions with the larger vision you've set. This is where many leaders falter—there's often a gap between what they say and what they do. To truly inspire and lead with vision, you must embody that vision every day.

Potential Challenges:

One challenge leaders face is staying consistent with their vision when under pressure. When the demands of day-to-day operations pile up, it can be easy to lose sight of the bigger picture. But this is exactly when your vision is most critical—it helps you make decisions that align with your long-term goals, even when faced with immediate challenges.

In the next chapters, we'll explore how vision ties into other leadership principles like building high-performing teams, cultivating emotional intelligence, and leading with integrity. But as you begin this journey, remember that vision is the foundation. It's what will guide you through challenges, inspire those around you, and ultimately determine your success as a leader.

Chapter 2: Principled Leadership

2.1 What It Means to Lead with Principles

The first time I realized the true meaning of principled leadership, I was in the midst of what felt like a defining career moment. I had been asked to make a decision that could have drastically affected the integrity of our company. It was a lucrative deal, one that promised impressive short-term gains. But something felt off. Deep down, I knew that pursuing this opportunity would compromise our core values. Yet, the pressure to act was overwhelming. We had investors breathing down our necks, and my team was expecting results.

In that moment, I had to pause and ask myself, "What do I really stand for? What are the non-negotiable principles that guide me as a leader?" This internal conversation set the foundation for my leadership journey and shaped the way I approached every decision after that. Leading with principles isn't about taking the easy or profitable path—it's about staying true to what you believe in, even when the stakes are high. That's when I truly understood the power of leading with principles.

2.1.1 Defining Principled Leadership

Principled leadership is about grounding your actions and decisions in a set of core, unwavering beliefs. These principles act as your compass, guiding you through uncertainty, challenges, and ethical dilemmas. Leading with principles establishes trust within your team because people know where you stand. They can rely on you to be consistent, to act with integrity, and to put the greater good above short-term gains.

I've seen how transformative this can be firsthand. When my team realized that I wasn't going to chase quick wins at the expense of our core values, something shifted. They knew they could trust me, and that trust translated into a deeper sense of loyalty and commitment. In an age where corporate scandals and ethical lapses seem all too common, principled leadership offers stability—a beacon of reliability in a turbulent world.

2.1.2 Principles vs. Tactics

Early in my career, I often confused principles with tactics. I thought that if I just mastered the right leadership strategies, I could achieve any outcome. But tactics are fluid; they change with the environment, the market, and the situation. Principles, on the other hand, are enduring. They don't change based on circumstances—they are the bedrock upon which successful, ethical leadership is built.

Take the case of a mentor I had in one of my first management roles. He was an incredibly tactical leader, always aware of the latest strategies to improve efficiency and profitability. But one day, when a difficult decision arose involving the well-being of some employees, he faltered. His tactics didn't give him the answers he needed, and without a solid foundation of principles, he made a decision that caused long-term damage to the team's trust.

That experience taught me a valuable lesson: while tactics can help you achieve short-term wins, principles are what sustain long-term success. Tactics evolve, but your principles must remain steadfast.

2.1.3 How Integrity Drives Influence

Integrity is the cornerstone of principled leadership. It's easy to think that influence comes from position or power, but the most influential leaders I've encountered are those who lead with integrity. When people know that you stand by your values, they're more likely to follow you—not because they have to, but because they want to.

One of the hardest decisions I had to make involved standing up for what I believed in, even when it wasn't the most popular choice. There were moments when it would have been easier to compromise my values for convenience or approval. But I knew that my integrity was worth more than any short-term gain. Over time, that commitment to integrity became the reason people trusted my leadership.

Leaders who act with integrity inspire loyalty and respect. They influence not by dictating orders, but by leading by example, showing their teams what it means to stay true to one's values. Integrity builds credibility, and credibility is the foundation of influence.

2.2 Identifying and Committing to Your Core Principles

Principled leadership begins with self-awareness. Before you can lead others with integrity, you must understand your own beliefs and values. This requires deep reflection—a process I went through during some of the most challenging times in my life. It was in those moments of struggle that I came face-to-face with my core principles, and it's that journey that I want to share with you.

2.2.1 Self-Reflection: Discovering Your Core Beliefs

To lead with principles, you must first know what those principles are. For me, this discovery didn't happen overnight. I had to engage in deep self-reflection, asking myself questions that weren't always easy to answer:

What do I truly stand for? What values are non-negotiable in my life and leadership?

One exercise that helped me was journaling about pivotal moments in my career—times when I felt most challenged, most proud, or most conflicted. In those moments, I was able to uncover the beliefs that drove my decisions. Was it a commitment to fairness? A belief in innovation? A desire to empower others? Identifying your core principles requires you to look at your past actions and ask yourself why you made the choices you did.

I encourage you to take time to reflect on your own journey. What values have consistently guided you, even when the road was difficult? The clearer you are about your core principles, the easier it becomes to lead with confidence and integrity.

2.2.2 Aligning Principles with Your Vision

Once you've identified your core principles, the next step is aligning them with your vision. Your principles should act as the foundation upon which your vision is built. Without alignment, you risk creating a vision that looks good on paper but doesn't resonate with who you are or what you believe.

In Chapter 1, we discussed how to craft a compelling vision. Now, let's take that a step further by ensuring that your vision is a true reflection of your principles. I've seen leaders create ambitious visions that failed because they weren't rooted in their core beliefs. Your team will sense it if your vision lacks authenticity, and they will struggle to buy into it.

In my own leadership journey, I found that when my vision was aligned with my principles, it became more powerful. It was no longer just a statement of intent—it was a natural extension of who I was as a leader. People could see that my actions and decisions were consistent with my values, which made them more willing to follow me on the path toward that vision.

2.2.3 Handling Conflicts and Dilemmas with Integrity

No matter how principled you are, there will be moments when you face conflicts and dilemmas that test your resolve. I've been in situations where two of my core principles seemed to be in direct conflict with one another. For example, how do you balance transparency with confidentiality? How do you uphold fairness while also pushing for high performance?

In those moments, it's easy to feel stuck or even paralyzed. But principled leadership isn't about avoiding difficult decisions—it's about making those decisions with integrity. I've found that when faced with these challenges, going back to my core principles helps me navigate the dilemma. It's not always about choosing the "right" answer, but about staying true to what you believe in and being willing to stand by your decisions.

2.3 Embodying Your Principles as a Leader

It's one thing to know your principles—it's another to live by them every day. The most successful and respected leaders are those who consistently embody their principles in their actions, even when it's inconvenient or uncomfortable.

2.3.1 Walking the Talk

Early in my leadership career, I made the mistake of thinking that as long as I articulated my values, my team would follow them. I quickly learned that words alone aren't enough. Your team will be watching how you act, not just what you say.

Walking the talk means embodying your principles in every decision you make, no matter how small. It means being consistent in your actions and showing your team that you practice what you preach. This was a lesson I learned when I had to make a tough decision about downsizing. I could have approached it with a cold, numbers-driven mindset, but my principles of empathy and fairness guided me to handle the situation with transparency and care. My team saw that, and it reinforced their trust in me.

2.3.2 Accountability and Transparency

One of the keys to principled leadership is creating systems for accountability. As leaders, we must not only hold ourselves accountable but also create an environment where others feel empowered to hold us accountable. In my experience, the most effective leaders are those who actively seek feedback and are transparent about their decision-making processes.

There was a time when I had to admit to my team that I had made a mistake. It wasn't easy, but by being transparent and taking accountability, I reinforced the principles of honesty and integrity that I had always preached. That moment of vulnerability actually strengthened my leadership because it showed my team that I was human, and more importantly, that I was committed to living my principles.

2.3.3 Mentoring and Leading by Example

One of the greatest privileges of leadership is the opportunity to mentor others. As leaders, we have the responsibility to not only embody our principles but also to teach others how to lead with integrity. Mentoring allows you to pass on the lessons you've learned and inspire the next generation of leaders to lead with purpose and conviction.

I've always believed that the best way to mentor is by example. When your team sees you consistently living your principles, they're more likely to follow suit. It's not about perfection—it's about authenticity. When you lead by example, you create a culture of integrity that extends beyond yourself and into the fabric of your organization.

In the next chapters, we'll dive deeper into how to build a culture that supports principled leadership, and how to navigate the challenges that arise when your principles are put to the test. But for now, remember this: leadership isn't about perfection. It's about progress. Leading with principles is a journey—one that requires constant reflection, adjustment, and commitment. As long as you stay true to your core beliefs, you'll continue to grow as a leader and inspire those around you to do the same.

Chapter 3: Building a Strategic Mindset

As I reflect on my leadership journey, one of the biggest shifts I had to make was learning to think strategically, rather than simply reacting to the challenges of the day. Early on, I was constantly putting out fires—racing from one problem to the next, feeling like I was always playing catch-up. It was exhausting and, worse, it wasn't effective. It wasn't until I learned how to move from reactive to proactive leadership that I started to make real progress, both in my career and in my ability to lead others.

I remember one day in particular that forced me to confront this. I had spent the better part of a week dealing with issues that felt urgent but, in hindsight, weren't actually important. At the end of that week, I found myself staring at a pile of unfinished work that truly mattered, and I realized that I hadn't moved the needle on anything substantial. I was busy, but I wasn't being effective. It was a wake-up call, and from that moment forward, I committed to developing a more strategic mindset.

Let's explore what it means to build that kind of mindset and how you can shift from reacting to challenges to proactively shaping your leadership and your future.

3.1 Shifting from Reactive to Proactive Leadership

3.1.1 Understanding the Importance of Strategy

In leadership, we often get caught up in the immediate. A crisis emerges, a deadline approaches, a key team member suddenly leaves—there's always something demanding our attention. And while dealing with these challenges is part of being a leader, the danger comes when we lose sight of the bigger picture. I've been there, and I know how easy it is to spend all your time reacting instead of stepping back to think strategically.

I remember leading a project where every day felt like a new fire to put out. The problem was, I wasn't thinking ahead—I was just reacting to whatever problem came my way. But true leadership isn't about firefighting; it's about looking beyond the immediate to ensure that today's actions contribute to tomorrow's goals. I had to learn that the best leaders prioritize strategy. They understand that without a clear vision and a plan to get there, they're just running in circles.

When I finally made the shift to strategic thinking, it transformed the way I led my team. Instead of reacting to problems, we began anticipating them. We started setting long-term goals, and more importantly, we took steps to achieve them. The immediate challenges didn't disappear, but we were able to face them with a clearer sense of purpose.

3.1.2 Identifying Reactive Patterns in Leadership

If you're like me, it can be difficult to recognize when you're stuck in a reactive leadership cycle. It's easy to justify being busy—there's always an email to answer, a meeting to attend, or a crisis to manage. But at some point, I realized that I wasn't actually moving toward my goals. I was just treading water.

One of the most common traps leaders fall into is mistaking busyness for productivity. I've had weeks where I worked nonstop but accomplished very little that aligned with my long-term vision. I was stuck in reactive patterns, putting out fires instead of taking control of my time and energy.

Think about your own leadership. Are you constantly reacting to problems that pop up? Do you find yourself scrambling at the last minute because you didn't take time to plan ahead? Identifying these patterns is the first step toward building a strategic mindset. Once I recognized how reactive I had become, I was able to make a conscious shift toward a more proactive approach.

3.1.3 Creating Space for Strategic Thinking

One of the biggest lessons I've learned is that if you want to be a strategic leader, you need to create space for strategic thinking. This doesn't just happen on its own—you have to be intentional about it. When I was in firefighting mode, I rarely took time to step back and reflect. I was so busy tackling immediate tasks that I didn't have the mental space to think about the bigger picture.

To build a strategic mindset, I started carving out regular time for planning and reflection. Whether it's setting aside an hour every week or dedicating one day a month, you need to prioritize this time. For me, it was about blocking off "thinking time" in my calendar, just as I would for a meeting. During this time, I would focus solely on long-term planning, setting goals, and assessing whether my current actions were aligned with my vision.

This practice was a game-changer. I found that when I made space for strategic thinking, I was able to make better decisions and avoid many of the crises that used to consume my days. I wasn't just reacting anymore—I was leading with purpose.

3.2 Setting Clear, Long-Term Objectives

3.2.1 Defining Long-Term vs. Short-Term Goals

As leaders, we often hear about the importance of setting goals, but not all goals are created equal. Early in my career, I made the mistake of focusing solely on short-term wins. I wanted to prove myself, so I set small, achievable goals that gave me quick results. And while those wins felt good in the moment, they weren't moving me closer to my bigger vision.

Over time, I learned the value of balancing short-term goals with long-term objectives. Short-term goals are important—they give you momentum and keep your team engaged—but if you don't have a long-term vision, you'll end up drifting without direction.

I remember a time when our company was experiencing rapid growth. It was exciting, but we were so focused on hitting immediate targets that we lost sight of our bigger mission. We were achieving short-term success, but it wasn't sustainable. We had to step back and redefine our long-term objectives, aligning them with our core values and vision. That shift helped us build a more sustainable path forward.

3.2.2 Setting SMART Strategic Goals

One of the most effective tools I've used in my leadership journey is the concept of SMART goals—Specific, Measurable, Achievable, Relevant, and Time-bound. This framework helped me move from vague aspirations to concrete, actionable steps. For example, instead of saying, "I want my team to be more efficient," I started setting goals like, "I want to reduce project timelines by 15% over the next six months by streamlining our processes."

The difference was striking. SMART goals gave me and my team a clear target to work toward, and they made it easier to measure our progress. When you set goals this way, you give yourself a roadmap to follow, which is essential for strategic leadership.

3.2.3 Breaking Down Big Goals into Achievable Steps

Once I started setting SMART goals, I quickly realized that achieving big, long-term objectives can feel overwhelming. I've seen this not just in myself but in the leaders I've mentored as well. You set this ambitious goal, and then you freeze because you don't know where to start.

The key is to break down those big goals into smaller, manageable steps. When I was leading a major initiative to restructure our company's operations, the end goal seemed daunting. But by breaking it down into smaller tasks—each with its own timeline and accountability—we were able to make steady progress.

I've found that this approach not only makes the process more manageable, but it also keeps the team motivated. Every small step forward is a win, and those wins build momentum toward the larger goal.

3.3 Staying Agile in a Changing Environment

3.3.1 Embracing Change and Uncertainty

One of the most important lessons I've learned in leadership is that change is inevitable. No matter how well you plan, the world around you is going to shift. I used to resist change—I wanted things to go according to plan. But the more I tried to control every outcome, the more frustrated I became.

Eventually, I realized that the most successful leaders aren't those who avoid change but those who embrace it. They see uncertainty as an opportunity rather than a threat. This shift in mindset allowed me to approach change with curiosity instead of fear. I began to ask myself, "How can this change help us grow? What opportunities does it present?"

3.3.2 Pivoting Without Losing Focus

While embracing change is essential, it's also important to maintain focus on your vision. I've seen leaders get so caught up in the excitement of new opportunities that they lose sight of their original goals. It's a delicate balance—staying agile enough to adapt while remaining committed to your long-term objectives.

There was a time when we were tempted to pivot our company's strategy to chase a trend in the industry. It seemed like the right move at the time, but as we started shifting resources and energy, I realized we were drifting away from our core mission. We had to course-correct and refocus on what mattered most. It was a tough lesson, but it reinforced the importance of staying aligned with your vision, even as you navigate change.

3.3.3 Continuous Learning and Adaptation

Finally, building a strategic mindset requires a commitment to continuous learning. The world is changing faster than ever, and as leaders, we have to stay curious and adaptable. I've made it a priority to seek out new knowledge, whether through reading, attending workshops, or learning from others in my field.

One of the most powerful ways I've learned is by surrounding myself with people who challenge me. I seek out mentors who push me to think differently, and I encourage my team to bring new ideas to the table. This culture of continuous learning keeps us agile and prepared to face whatever challenges come our way.

In the next chapters, we'll delve deeper into how to build a culture that supports strategic thinking and agility. But for now, remember that building a strategic mindset is a journey. It requires reflection, planning, and the ability to stay open to change. By shifting from reactive to proactive leadership, setting clear long-term goals, and staying agile, you'll position yourself—and your team—for lasting success.

Chapter 4: Emotional Intelligence in Leadership

I'll never forget the day I realized how much I had to learn about emotional intelligence. It was early in my career, and I was leading a project that had hit a roadblock. My team was frustrated, and I could feel the tension mounting in every meeting. My instinct was to push harder—after all, we had deadlines to meet and targets to hit. But what I didn't see at the time was that my approach was making the situation worse. Instead of motivating my team, I was shutting them down.

That all changed during a conversation with one of my colleagues, someone who had always been a quiet observer but was deeply respected by the team. After one particularly tense meeting, he pulled me aside and said, "You know, if you spent a little more time listening, really listening, you might see that people aren't just frustrated with the project—they're feeling overwhelmed, unheard, and burned out." His words stung, but they were exactly what I needed to hear. I wasn't connecting with my team on an emotional level, and that disconnect was eroding trust.

That moment became a turning point for me. It forced me to recognize the power of emotional intelligence (EQ) in leadership. I had always thought leadership was about having the right strategy, making tough decisions, and driving results. And while those things are important, I learned that they are only part of the equation. Leading effectively also means understanding people—knowing how to inspire them, how to support them, and how to navigate the emotional landscape of your team.

In this chapter, we're going to dive deep into emotional intelligence and its role in leadership. I'll share some of my personal experiences, and we'll explore how you can develop and apply emotional intelligence to become a more effective, compassionate, and inspiring leader.

4.1 The Foundation of Emotional Intelligence (EQ)

4.1.1 Defining Emotional Intelligence

Emotional intelligence is often defined as the ability to recognize, understand, manage, and influence our own emotions and the emotions of others. It's made up of four key components: self-awareness, self-regulation, empathy, and social skills. Each of these elements plays a crucial role in leadership, and together, they form the foundation of emotionally intelligent leadership.

For me, the real power of emotional intelligence became clear when I realized that people aren't just motivated by logic or incentives—they are driven by how they feel. If you can connect with people on an emotional level, you can inspire them to do their best work, even in challenging circumstances. On the flip side, if you ignore the emotional undercurrents within your team, it can lead to disengagement, resentment, and ultimately, poor performance.

Understanding emotional intelligence helped me transform my approach to leadership. I began to see that leadership isn't just about managing tasks; it's about managing emotions—both mine and those of the people I lead.

4.1.2 Self-Awareness: Knowing Your Strengths and Weaknesses

Self-awareness is the cornerstone of emotional intelligence. It's about understanding who you are—your strengths, your weaknesses, your triggers, and your blind spots. For a long time, I thought I was self-aware. I prided myself on being confident and decisive, but I was missing a key element: understanding how my emotions and behaviors were affecting the people around me.

One of the hardest lessons I had to learn was that my strengths as a leader could also be my weaknesses. My drive to succeed sometimes made me impatient, and my confidence could come off as arrogance. I wasn't always aware of how my actions were being perceived, and that lack of self-awareness was creating barriers between me and my team.

I remember a time when we were in the middle of a high-stakes project, and I was so focused on hitting our goals that I became laser-focused on tasks. I didn't realize that my intensity was making people feel like they couldn't voice their concerns. I was leading from a place of pressure, not empathy. When I finally took a step back and asked for feedback, I was shocked at what I heard. My team felt that I wasn't approachable, that I wasn't listening to their ideas, and that they were afraid to speak up.

That experience taught me the importance of self-awareness. I started paying closer attention to how I was showing up as a leader. I made it a habit to reflect on my actions and ask for feedback regularly. This not only helped me grow, but it also made my team feel more comfortable being honest with me, which improved our working relationships and overall performance.

4.1.3 Empathy: Connecting with Others on a Deeper Level

If self-awareness is the first step to emotional intelligence, empathy is the second. Empathy is about understanding and sharing the feelings of others. It's the ability to put yourself in someone else's shoes and see the world from their perspective. In leadership, empathy is what allows you to connect with your team on a deeper level, build trust, and inspire loyalty.

I've found that empathy is especially important during times of stress and uncertainty. I remember a time when we were going through a major organizational restructuring. The team was anxious about their jobs, their roles, and their future. My first instinct was to focus on the logistics—communicating the plan, outlining the new structure, and ensuring we stayed on track. But I quickly realized that what people needed most in that moment wasn't a strategy—it was empathy. They needed to know that I understood their fears and concerns and that I was there to support them through the transition.

By taking the time to listen to their worries and acknowledge their emotions, I was able to build a stronger sense of trust. People felt heard, and that made all the difference in how they responded to the changes. Empathy isn't about fixing people's problems—it's about being there with them, showing that you care, and helping them navigate challenges with confidence.

4.2 Developing Your EQ as a Leader

4.2.1 Cultivating Self-Regulation

Self-regulation is the ability to manage your emotions, especially in stressful or challenging situations. As leaders, we're often under pressure to make tough decisions, meet tight deadlines, and navigate conflict. It's easy to let emotions like frustration, anger, or anxiety take over. But as I've learned, how we handle our emotions in these moments sets the tone for the entire team.

Early in my career, I had a tendency to react quickly when things didn't go as planned. If a meeting went off track or a project hit a snag, my frustration would show—whether through my tone of voice, my body language, or my impatience. I didn't realize how much those reactions were affecting the people around me. When I wasn't able to regulate my emotions, my team felt on edge, and it created a culture of stress and fear.

Over time, I learned the importance of self-regulation. I began practicing mindfulness techniques to help me stay calm under pressure. I started pausing before reacting, giving myself a moment to process the situation before responding. This not only helped me manage my own emotions, but it also created a more composed and resilient environment for my team.

4.2.2 Mastering Social Awareness

Social awareness is the ability to read and understand the emotions of others. It's about picking up on the subtle cues that people give through their body language, tone of voice, and behavior. I've found that leaders who are socially aware are able to build stronger teams because they can sense when something is off and address it before it becomes a bigger issue.

I once worked with a manager who was incredibly skilled at reading the room. During meetings, she had a way of sensing when someone wasn't speaking up or when there was tension in the air. She would pause the conversation and ask, "What's going on? I feel like there's something we're not addressing." Her ability to tune into the emotional dynamics of the team made her a highly effective leader. People trusted her because they knew she was paying attention, not just to the work, but to the people doing the work.

I've tried to model that same level of social awareness in my own leadership. By paying closer attention to how people are feeling and what they're not saying, I've been able to build stronger, more cohesive teams.

4.2.3 Using EQ to Navigate Difficult Conversations

One of the most challenging aspects of leadership is having difficult conversations—whether it's giving critical feedback, addressing a conflict, or delivering tough news. In the past, I dreaded these conversations. I would avoid them, hoping the problem would resolve itself. But, of course, it never did.

I've since learned that emotional intelligence is key to navigating difficult conversations effectively. The first step is to approach the conversation with empathy—understanding how the other person might be feeling and acknowledging their perspective. Next, it's about regulating your own emotions so that you can stay calm and focused, even when the conversation gets tough. Finally, it's about being clear, honest, and compassionate in your communication.

I remember a time when I had to let a team member go. It was one of the hardest conversations I've ever had. But because I approached it with empathy and emotional intelligence, the conversation, while difficult, was also respectful and compassionate. We were able to part on good terms, and that experience reinforced for me the importance of leading with emotional intelligence.

4.3 Leveraging EQ for Team Success

4.3.1 Building a Culture of Trust and Emotional Safety

One of the most powerful things emotionally intelligent leaders can do is create a culture of trust and emotional safety. When people feel safe to express themselves, share their ideas, and take risks, they are more engaged, more creative, and more productive.

I've worked in environments where trust was lacking, and it stifled innovation. People were afraid to speak up or offer new ideas because they feared criticism or rejection. Conversely, I've also been part of teams where trust and emotional safety were prioritized, and the difference was night and day. People were willing to take bold risks because they knew they wouldn't be punished for failing. Instead, they would be supported in their growth and learning.

As a leader, I strive to create that kind of environment for my teams. I make it a point to listen without judgment, encourage open communication, and celebrate both successes and failures as opportunities for growth.

4.3.2 Enhancing Collaboration and Communication

Emotional intelligence also plays a key role in fostering collaboration and communication. When leaders are emotionally intelligent, they create an environment where people feel comfortable working together, sharing ideas, and supporting one another.

I've seen firsthand how emotional intelligence can enhance collaboration. On one project, we had a team of highly skilled individuals, but they weren't communicating effectively. There were misunderstandings, misaligned priorities, and a general sense of frustration. I realized that the issue wasn't their technical abilities—it was a lack of emotional connection. By focusing on building trust, improving communication, and fostering empathy within the team, we were able to turn things around. The team became more cohesive, and our performance improved significantly.

4.3.3 Inspiring and Motivating Others with EQ

Finally, emotional intelligence is key to inspiring and motivating others. People are motivated not just by what you say, but by how you make them feel. As a leader, your ability to connect with people on an emotional level—through empathy, compassion, and self-awareness—can inspire them to reach their full potential.

I've found that the most inspiring leaders aren't necessarily the ones with the best strategies or the most knowledge. They're the ones who make you feel seen, heard, and valued. They're the leaders who understand your struggles, celebrate your successes, and challenge you to grow.

In my own leadership journey, I've made it a priority to lead with emotional intelligence. By doing so, I've been able to build stronger teams, create more meaningful connections, and inspire the people around me to achieve their best. And that, to me, is what leadership is all about.

Chapter 5: Influence and Persuasion: The Art of Guiding Others

There's a moment in every leader's journey when you realize that being in charge isn't the same as being influential. I learned this lesson the hard way. Early in my career, I believed that having authority was enough to get things done. I thought that if I had the title, people would naturally follow. But I quickly discovered that people don't follow titles—they follow leaders who inspire, connect, and persuade.

I was managing a team of highly skilled professionals, and we were working on a major project with tight deadlines. I assumed that because I was the one in charge, the team would automatically buy into my vision and follow my lead. But despite my best efforts, the team wasn't fully engaged. I could sense resistance, and it was clear that something wasn't clicking. I had the authority, but I wasn't influencing them in the way I needed to.

It wasn't until I started focusing on influence, rather than authority, that things began to change. I realized that leadership is about more than just making decisions and giving directions—it's about building relationships, earning trust, and guiding others in a way that inspires them to take action. Influence is subtle, but powerful, and it's something that must be earned over time. In this chapter, we'll explore how to cultivate influence and master the art of persuasion, so that you can guide others effectively, whether you have formal authority or not.

5.1 Understanding Influence vs. Authority

5.1.1 The Difference Between Influence and Power

One of the most important lessons I've learned in leadership is the distinction between influence and power. Early in my career, I thought that having power meant having control. I believed that if I had the authority, people would listen, follow, and do what was asked. But I quickly realized that power without influence is hollow.

I remember leading a team meeting where I outlined our next steps for a major initiative. I was confident in my plan and expected everyone to jump on board. But as I looked around the room, I could tell that people weren't fully engaged. They nodded along, but their body language told a different story—they were disconnected, not bought in. I had the power to direct them, but I lacked the influence to truly inspire them.

That moment was a wake-up call for me. I realized that true leadership isn't about issuing orders—it's about inspiring action. Influence is far more sustainable and effective than traditional authority because it's rooted in relationships, not mandates. Influence is earned through trust, respect, and mutual understanding. It's not something you can demand; it's something you must cultivate.

5.1.2 Building Trust as the Foundation of Influence

The foundation of influence is trust. Without trust, you can't guide people in a meaningful way. Trust takes time to build, and it's easily lost, but when you have it, you can move mountains. One of the key moments in my leadership journey was when I learned how to build trust with my team. I realized that trust wasn't just about being honest—it was about being consistent, reliable, and showing that I genuinely cared about their success.

There was a time when one of my team members came to me with a problem they were struggling with, and I was tempted to give a quick solution and move on. But something told me to slow down and really listen. I asked questions, empathized with their situation, and worked with them to come up with a solution that felt right for them. That conversation deepened the trust between us, and from that point on, they were more engaged, more open, and more willing to go the extra mile for the team.

Trust isn't built in a single moment, but in many small interactions over time. It's built when people see that you're consistent in your values, that you follow through on your commitments, and that you genuinely care about their well-being. When people trust you, they're more willing to be influenced by you because they know you have their best interests at heart.

5.1.3 The Role of Reciprocity in Influence

Reciprocity is one of the most powerful principles of influence. When you give to others—whether it's your time, support, or expertise—they are naturally inclined to give back. I've seen this play out time and time again in my career. When I've gone out of my way to help others, even when it wasn't directly related to my goals, I found that people were far more willing to support me when I needed it.

I remember a time when I was working on a project that required cross-departmental collaboration. There was one department head who was notoriously difficult to work with. Many of my colleagues had warned me that getting their support would be nearly impossible. But instead of approaching them with a request, I decided to take a different approach. I spent time understanding their challenges and offered my help on a project they were struggling with. I didn't ask for anything in return—my goal was simply to be of service.

A few weeks later, when I needed their support for my project, they were more than willing to help. The principle of reciprocity had kicked in. By helping them first, I had earned their willingness to reciprocate. Influence isn't about manipulation—it's about building mutually beneficial relationships where both parties are invested in each other's success.

5.2 Mastering Persuasion Techniques

5.2.1 The Power of Persuasive Communication

One of the most important skills you can develop as a leader is the ability to communicate persuasively. I used to think that being persuasive meant being forceful or convincing people through sheer logic. But over time, I learned that persuasion is more about how you make people feel than the facts you present.

I remember a time when I had to pitch a new initiative to senior leadership. I had all the data to back up my proposal, and I was confident in my numbers. But as I began my presentation, I could sense that the room wasn't fully engaged. I realized that while my data was solid, I wasn't connecting with them on an emotional level.

So, I changed my approach. Instead of leading with the numbers, I shared a story about a customer who had been impacted by our product. I talked about the challenges they were facing and how our new initiative could help solve their problems. As I told the story, I could see the shift in the room. People were leaning in, nodding along, and by the time I got to the data, they were already convinced. They weren't just buying into the numbers—they were buying into the emotional connection.

Persuasive communication is about tapping into both the head and the heart. It's about finding the balance between logic and emotion and using both to inspire action.

5.2.2 Using Data and Stories for Persuasion

One of the most effective ways to persuade others is by combining data with storytelling. Data provides the logic and credibility, while stories create an emotional connection. I've found that when you can weave these two elements together, your message becomes far more compelling.

For example, when I was leading a major initiative to overhaul our customer service process, I knew I needed to get buy-in from multiple stakeholders. I had plenty of data to show why the changes were necessary—response times were too slow, customer satisfaction was dropping, and we were losing business. But I also knew that data alone wouldn't be enough to move people.

So, I shared a story about a long-time customer who had grown frustrated with our service. I talked about how they had been loyal to us for years, but recently had started looking at competitors because they felt like we weren't listening to their needs. That story brought the data to life. Suddenly, the numbers weren't just abstract statistics—they represented real people with real experiences. By the end of the presentation, everyone was on board with the changes.

Data and stories are a powerful combination because they appeal to both logic and emotion. When you can use both effectively, you can persuade people in a way that feels genuine and impactful.

5.2.3 Tailoring Your Message to Different Audiences

One of the most important lessons I've learned about persuasion is that there's no one-size-fits-all approach. Different audiences have different needs, values, and concerns, and it's essential to tailor your message accordingly. What resonates with one group may fall flat with another, so it's important to understand who you're speaking to and what matters most to them.

I've had experiences where I delivered the same message to two different groups, only to get completely different reactions. In one instance, I was presenting a new strategic direction to my team. I focused on the big picture and how the new strategy would help us achieve our long-term goals. The team was excited, motivated, and ready to get started. But when I presented the same message to senior leadership, the response was lukewarm at best. They were more concerned about the immediate impact on operations and how we would manage the transition.

I quickly realized that I hadn't tailored my message to the concerns of senior leadership. They needed to see a detailed plan that addressed the short-term challenges, not just the long-term vision. Once I adjusted my approach, focusing on the operational impact and how we would mitigate risks, their support came quickly.

Tailoring your message is about understanding the priorities of your audience and framing your communication in a way that speaks to those priorities. It's about meeting people where they are, not where you want them to be.

5.3 Expanding Your Sphere of Influence

5.3.1 Building Networks of Influence

As a leader, one of the most powerful things you can do is build a network of influence. No one leads alone, and your ability to get things done often depends on the relationships you've built. I've found that the most influential leaders are the ones who take the time to cultivate relationships—not just with people in their immediate circle, but across the organization and beyond.

Early in my career, I made the mistake of focusing too narrowly on my own team. I worked hard to build strong relationships with the people I worked with directly, but I didn't put as much effort into building connections with other departments or external partners. It wasn't until I needed support from other areas of the organization that I realized the importance of having a broader network.

I started making a conscious effort to build relationships with people outside of my immediate team. I volunteered for cross-functional projects, attended networking events, and made it a point to reach out to colleagues in other departments. Over time, those relationships became invaluable. When I needed help, I had a network of people who were willing to support me because I had invested in them first.

Building a network of influence isn't about making transactional connections—it's about building genuine relationships based on trust, mutual respect, and shared goals.

5.3.2 Influencing Up, Down, and Across the Organization

One of the challenges of leadership is that you need to influence people at all levels of the organization. You need to guide your team, collaborate with peers, and influence senior leaders—all while staying aligned with your vision and values. I've found that influencing across the organization requires a different set of skills than just leading a team. It's about being adaptable, understanding the needs and concerns of different stakeholders, and finding common ground.

There was a time when I was leading a project that required buy-in from multiple departments. Each department had its own priorities, and getting everyone on the same page was a challenge. I quickly realized that I couldn't take a one-size-fits-all approach. I needed to understand the unique concerns of each group and tailor my message accordingly.

For my team, I focused on how the project aligned with our long-term goals and how it would benefit them in their day-to-day work. For senior leadership, I highlighted the strategic impact and how the project would drive business growth. For my peers in other departments, I emphasized how the project would help them achieve their own objectives. By tailoring my message to each audience, I was able to build support across the organization and get everyone moving in the same direction.

Influencing up, down, and across the organization requires flexibility, empathy, and the ability to see things from different perspectives. It's about finding common ground and aligning everyone's goals with the larger vision.

5.3.3 Developing Influence Beyond Your Organization

As a leader, your influence shouldn't stop at the walls of your organization. One of the most rewarding aspects of leadership is using your influence to create positive change in your industry and community. I've found that some of the most impactful leaders are those who use their platform to advocate for causes they believe in, mentor others, and contribute to the greater good.

Early in my career, I had the opportunity to mentor a group of young professionals through a leadership development program. At first, I wasn't sure if I had the time or experience to make a meaningful impact. But as I got to know the participants and saw how eager they were to learn and grow, I realized that mentoring was one of the most powerful ways I could expand my influence beyond my immediate role.

Mentoring isn't just about sharing your knowledge—it's about investing in the next generation of leaders and helping them achieve their full potential. It's about using your influence to lift others up and create a ripple effect of positive change.

By developing influence beyond your organization, you not only make a difference in the lives of others, but you also expand your own leadership capacity. You become a leader who is not just focused on personal success, but on creating lasting impact in the world around you.

In leadership, influence and persuasion are not just tools—they are art forms that, when mastered, can transform your ability to guide others. By focusing on building trust, communicating persuasively, and expanding your sphere of influence, you can lead with impact, inspire lasting change, and create a legacy of positive influence that extends far beyond your immediate role.

Chapter 6: Building High-Performing Teams

One of the most rewarding aspects of leadership is building a team that not only works well together but also thrives. In my experience, the strength of a leader is not measured by their own achievements, but by the success of the team they build. I've been fortunate to lead several high-performing teams throughout my career, but it wasn't always smooth sailing. There were times when we struggled with accountability, communication, and alignment. But by focusing on creating a culture of ownership, setting clear objectives, and fostering leadership growth, we were able to turn things around.

In this chapter, I want to share the lessons I've learned about building high-performing teams. These are principles that, when applied, can transform a group of individuals into a unified, empowered team that's aligned with a shared vision and capable of achieving extraordinary results.

6.1 Creating a Culture of Accountability and Ownership

6.1.1 The Importance of Accountability in Team Success

I remember one particular project where accountability was the key to our success. We were working on a high-stakes product launch that required collaboration from multiple departments. In the early stages, it became clear that tasks were slipping through the cracks. Deadlines were missed, and people were pointing fingers. It wasn't that my team lacked talent—far from it. But we were missing a culture of accountability, and without that, even the best teams will struggle.

I called a meeting and laid everything out on the table. We talked about the importance of accountability, not as a form of micromanagement, but as a way to ensure that each person could rely on the others. We agreed that going forward, every task would have a clear owner and deadline, and we committed to holding each other accountable in a constructive way.

From that point on, there was a noticeable shift. People took pride in their responsibilities and were more proactive about sharing progress or asking for help when needed. We delivered the project on time, and it was one of the most successful launches the company had seen. Accountability wasn't just about meeting deadlines—it fostered a sense of ownership and pride in our work, which led to better results across the board.

6.1.2 Empowering Your Team to Take Initiative

One of the hardest lessons I had to learn as a leader was letting go of control. Early on, I felt responsible for every decision, every detail, and every outcome. But as the team grew, it became impossible to manage everything myself. I had to learn to trust my team to step up, take initiative, and make decisions on their own.

There was one particular project where I was stretched too thin, and I knew I couldn't be as hands-on as I usually was. Instead of micromanaging, I empowered my team to take the lead. I told them, "This is your project now. I trust you to make the right decisions. If you need support, I'm here, but I want you to take ownership."

At first, there were some growing pains. People were hesitant, unsure if they had the authority to make certain decisions. But over time, they began to embrace the responsibility. They started coming up with creative solutions, collaborating more effectively, and owning their part of the project. The end result wasn't just a successful project—it was a stronger, more confident team that knew they had the ability to lead without constant oversight.

Empowering your team to take initiative is one of the best things you can do as a leader. It not only lightens your load but also helps your team members grow into leaders themselves.

6.1.3 Building a Feedback-Rich Environment

In my experience, the teams that perform the best are the ones that have a culture of open, constructive feedback. But I'll be honest—getting to that point wasn't easy. Early in my career, feedback was something people dreaded. It was only given during performance reviews or when something went wrong, and as a result, it often felt negative or punitive.

I realized that if we were going to improve as a team, feedback needed to be a regular, positive part of our culture. I started by changing the way I gave feedback. Instead of waiting for formal reviews, I made it a point to give feedback in real time, focusing not just on areas for improvement but also on what people were doing well. I encouraged my team to do the same with each other.

At first, people were hesitant. Giving and receiving feedback felt uncomfortable. But over time, it became second nature. We built a feedback-rich environment where people weren't afraid to speak up because they knew that feedback was about growth, not criticism. This culture of feedback helped us identify problems early, improve our processes, and ultimately become a more cohesive and high-performing team.

6.2 Aligning Team Goals with Organizational Vision

6.2.1 Creating Clear Roles and Responsibilities

One of the biggest challenges in leading a team is ensuring that everyone knows how their work contributes to the bigger picture. I've been in situations where team members were working hard, but their efforts weren't aligned with the overall vision of the organization. This lack of clarity led to frustration and inefficiency.

I'll never forget a particular project where we were falling behind on our deadlines despite everyone working long hours. I realized that part of the problem was that people weren't clear on their roles and how their work fit into the larger goals of the organization. Some were duplicating efforts, while others were unsure of what was expected of them.

We took a step back and clarified each person's role, ensuring that everyone understood how their work aligned with the organizational vision. We also made sure that each person's responsibilities were clear and that they knew who to turn to for support. The difference was immediate. Not only did we get back on track, but the team felt more engaged and motivated because they could see how their contributions were making a difference.

Creating clear roles and responsibilities is essential for aligning team efforts with the broader vision. It helps people feel connected to the bigger picture and ensures that everyone is working toward the same goals.

6.2.2 Setting Team Objectives that Inspire Commitment

Setting goals for the team is one thing—but setting goals that inspire true commitment is another. I've seen teams where goals were set in a vacuum, and while they might have been achievable, they didn't inspire passion or dedication. Without a strong connection to the "why" behind the goal, people were just going through the motions.

On one project, I decided to approach goal-setting differently. Instead of simply handing down objectives, I involved the team in the process. We talked about the overall vision of the organization and how our work contributed to that. Then, we collaborated to set team goals that not only aligned with the company's objectives but also resonated with each person's individual passions and strengths.

The difference was night and day. When the team was involved in setting the goals, they felt a sense of ownership and commitment that hadn't been there before. They weren't just working to meet a target—they were working toward something they believed in. This inspired commitment translated into higher performance and a deeper sense of purpose.

6.2.3 Fostering Collaboration and Innovation

One of the things I'm most proud of as a leader is fostering a team culture where collaboration and innovation thrive. But I'll admit, it wasn't always that way. There was a time when people worked in silos, focused on their individual tasks, and rarely collaborated across departments. As a result, we missed out on a lot of great ideas.

I knew that if we were going to build a truly high-performing team, we needed to break down those silos and create an environment where people felt encouraged to collaborate and innovate. I started by creating opportunities for cross-functional collaboration. We held brainstorming sessions where people from different departments could come together to solve problems and share ideas.

I also made it clear that innovation was a priority. We celebrated creative ideas and encouraged people to take risks, even if it meant failing sometimes. By fostering a culture of collaboration and innovation, we not only improved our processes but also came up with solutions that we never would have thought of if we had stayed in our silos.

6.3 Developing Future Leaders

6.3.1 Identifying and Nurturing Talent

One of the most fulfilling aspects of leadership is identifying and nurturing the future leaders within your team. I've always believed that part of my role as a leader is to help others grow into leadership roles themselves. But identifying talent isn't always straightforward. I've learned that the most promising leaders aren't always the loudest or most obvious choices.

I remember one team member who was quiet and reserved, but their work was consistently excellent. While they didn't speak up in meetings often, when they did, their insights were thoughtful and valuable. I began to notice their natural ability to lead by example, even if they weren't the most vocal person in the room. I made it a point to give them more responsibility and opportunities to lead smaller projects. Over time, their confidence grew, and they became one of the most effective leaders on the team.

Identifying future leaders means looking beyond the obvious and paying attention to the qualities that make a great leader—integrity, empathy, and the ability to inspire others. Once you've identified potential leaders, it's important to nurture their development through mentorship and opportunities for growth.

6.3.2 Mentorship and Leadership Development

Mentorship has played a critical role in my own development as a leader, and it's something I'm passionate about providing for others. I've had the privilege of mentoring several team members over the years, and I've seen firsthand how mentorship can accelerate leadership development.

One of my most rewarding experiences was mentoring a team member who had a lot of potential but lacked confidence in their leadership abilities. We worked together on developing their skills, focusing on areas like communication, decision-making, and conflict resolution. I also made sure to give them opportunities to take on leadership roles in small, low-risk situations where they could practice and build their confidence.

Over time, I watched them grow into a confident and capable leader. They took on more responsibility, and eventually, they were leading their own team. Seeing their growth was one of the most rewarding experiences of my career.

6.3.3 Creating Opportunities for Leadership Growth

One of the best ways to develop future leaders is by giving them opportunities to lead. This doesn't mean throwing them into the deep end without support—it means providing them with opportunities to practice leadership in a structured, supportive environment.

In my experience, one of the most effective ways to do this is by creating leadership development programs within the team. These programs can involve rotating leadership roles, where team members take turns leading meetings or small projects. It can also involve shadowing more experienced leaders or participating in cross-functional teams where they can develop their leadership skills in a collaborative setting.

Creating opportunities for leadership growth not only benefits the individuals who are developing their skills but also strengthens the entire team. It creates a culture of continuous learning and growth, where everyone is encouraged to step up and lead in their own way.

Building high-performing teams is not just about hiring the best talent or setting ambitious goals—it's about creating a culture where accountability, ownership, collaboration, and leadership development are prioritized. By focusing on these principles, you can build a team that not only meets but exceeds expectations, delivering exceptional results while fostering personal and professional growth.

Chapter 7: Resilience and Adaptability in Leadership

Resilience and adaptability aren't just buzzwords for leaders—they're essential qualities that separate great leaders from the rest. In my experience, the ability to persevere through setbacks and adapt to changing circumstances has made all the difference in my leadership journey. I've faced moments where everything seemed to be falling apart, but it was resilience that allowed me to push through, and adaptability that gave me the tools to pivot when things didn't go as planned.

I know firsthand how important it is to build these traits, and I also know that it doesn't happen overnight. It takes practice, self-awareness, and, sometimes, a few hard knocks to develop the mental and emotional fortitude to not just survive but thrive in leadership. In this chapter, I'm going to walk you through the lessons I've learned about resilience and adaptability—how to develop them within yourself, and how to foster these qualities in your team.

7.1 The Role of Resilience in Leadership

7.1.1 Why Resilience is Essential for Leaders

I've often thought about a time early in my career when I felt like giving up. It was during a project that seemed doomed from the start. Deadlines were slipping, key stakeholders were disengaged, and everything we tried seemed to hit a roadblock. I remember sitting in my office late one night, feeling completely overwhelmed, wondering if I had made a mistake in taking on this leadership role.

But then I thought about the team that was depending on me. I realized that if I gave up, they might too. That's when I made the decision to keep pushing, no matter how difficult things became. I didn't have all the answers, but I committed to staying in the fight.

Resilience is essential because leadership is often filled with unexpected challenges. No matter how well you plan, there will always be obstacles—whether it's a sudden market shift, a personal crisis, or a team issue that seems impossible to solve. The key is not to avoid challenges but to face them head-on with the understanding that setbacks are part of the journey. Resilience allows you to keep going when others might falter, and it sets the tone for your team to do the same.

7.1.2 Developing Mental Toughness

Over the years, I've found that mental toughness is a muscle that gets stronger with use. It's not something you're born with—it's something you develop through experience, reflection, and consistent effort.

One moment that helped me develop mental toughness was during a particularly difficult period when I was juggling multiple high-stakes projects at once. There were days when it felt like the pressure was too much, and I was on the verge of burnout. But instead of giving in, I took a step back and asked myself, "What can I control in this situation? What can I do right now to make progress?"

This shift in mindset—from focusing on what was going wrong to what I could actively do—was a game changer. I started breaking down tasks into smaller, more manageable steps and focused on making incremental progress. I also made a conscious effort to maintain a positive outlook, even when things weren't going well. This practice of staying present and taking control of what I could helped me develop the mental toughness needed to handle future challenges with more confidence and clarity.

7.1.3 Building Emotional Resilience

As a leader, you're not just dealing with tasks and deadlines—you're managing emotions, both your own and your team's. Emotional resilience is what allows you to maintain optimism, stay grounded, and keep your team motivated, even in the toughest times.

I remember leading a team through a particularly challenging phase where everything seemed to be going wrong. Morale was low, and I could feel the weight of everyone's stress and frustration. It would have been easy to let that negativity affect me, but I knew that my emotional state would set the tone for the team. So, I made a conscious effort to stay calm, to listen to their concerns without getting defensive, and to remind everyone of the bigger picture.

That experience taught me the importance of emotional resilience—of being able to manage your emotions under pressure. It's not about pretending everything is fine, but about acknowledging challenges while maintaining a sense of control and optimism. When you model emotional resilience, you show your team that it's possible to navigate tough times with grace and confidence, which in turn helps them stay grounded as well.

7.2 Cultivating Adaptability in a Changing World

7.2.1 Why Adaptability is the Key to Long-Term Success

The world is changing faster than ever. New technologies, shifting market conditions, and unexpected global events can completely transform the landscape in which we operate. As a leader, your ability to adapt is what will determine your long-term success.

I learned this lesson during a time when my team was focused on a particular product line that had been our bread and butter for years. We had a solid customer base, and everything seemed to be going well. But then, almost overnight, the market shifted. A new competitor came in with a more innovative, cost-effective solution, and suddenly, we were losing ground fast.

At first, we tried to double down on what had always worked in the past. But it quickly became clear that we couldn't win by sticking to the old ways. That's when we made the decision to pivot. We started looking at emerging trends and customer needs that we hadn't previously considered. We reallocated resources, revamped our strategy, and within a few months, we had launched a new product line that not only met the market's new demands but also positioned us as an industry leader once again.

That experience reinforced the importance of adaptability. No matter how successful you are today, things can change in an instant. The leaders who thrive in the long term are the ones who can adapt quickly and pivot when necessary.

7.2.2 Fostering an Adaptable Team Culture

Adaptability isn't just something you need to develop as a leader—it's something you need to foster within your team. One of the ways I've done this is by encouraging a culture of experimentation and continuous improvement. Instead of sticking rigidly to the way things have always been done, I challenge my team to think creatively, take risks, and come up with new ways to solve problems.

I remember a time when we were working on a particularly complex project, and nothing seemed to be going right. Our usual approaches weren't working, and the team was getting frustrated. Instead of pushing them to stick to the original plan, I encouraged them to take a step back and brainstorm new solutions. I made it clear that it was okay to fail, as long as we were learning and adapting along the way.

That shift in mindset made all the difference. The team came up with a completely new approach that not only solved the problem but also opened up new opportunities for growth. By fostering an adaptable culture, we were able to turn a difficult situation into a success.

7.2.3 Using Setbacks as Opportunities for Growth

One of the most important lessons I've learned as a leader is that setbacks are inevitable. But instead of seeing them as failures, I've learned to view them as opportunities for growth. Every setback is a chance to learn, improve, and come back stronger.

I'll never forget the time we were working on a project that completely fell apart. We had invested months of work, and it felt like a huge loss. At first, I was devastated. But after taking some time to reflect, I realized that this setback was actually an opportunity to learn. We took a hard look at what went wrong, what we could have done differently, and how we could improve going forward.

As a result, we came up with new processes and strategies that made us more efficient and effective in the future. That setback, as painful as it was at the time, ultimately made us a stronger team.

As a leader, your ability to turn setbacks into learning opportunities is one of the most valuable skills you can develop. It's not about avoiding failure—it's about using failure as a stepping stone to future success.

In leadership, resilience and adaptability are not optional—they are essential. Challenges will come, and the landscape will shift. The question is not whether you will face adversity, but how you will respond when it comes. By building resilience, both mentally and emotionally, and cultivating adaptability in yourself and your team, you'll be equipped to not only survive but thrive in an ever-changing world.

As you move forward in your leadership journey, remember that the road will not always be smooth. There will be times when you feel overwhelmed, when setbacks seem insurmountable, and when change feels like a constant uphill battle. But it's in those moments that your true leadership is tested and where your greatest growth happens.

Resilience and adaptability are not just traits—they are mindsets. They are the belief that no matter what happens, you have the strength, creativity, and flexibility to find a way forward. And when you embrace that mindset, there's nothing you and your team can't achieve.

Chapter 8: Leaving a Lasting Legacy

When I first started thinking about my leadership legacy, the concept seemed abstract. I was caught up in the day-to-day grind of meeting deadlines, managing teams, and achieving short-term goals. But over time, as I became more intentional in my leadership, I realized that everything I did—every decision, every conversation, every choice—was contributing to the legacy I was leaving behind.

A legacy isn't just about the accomplishments we accumulate in our careers. It's about the impact we have on others—the ripple effects of our leadership long after we've moved on. As I reflect on my journey, I see that leaving a lasting legacy requires more than just personal success. It's about empowering others, creating systems for continuous growth, and ensuring that the values you hold dear continue to influence the organization and people around you. In this chapter, I'll share my personal experiences and the lessons I've learned about building a leadership legacy that endures.

8.1 Defining Your Leadership Legacy

8.1.1 What Does a Legacy of Leadership Mean?

Early in my career, I thought of leadership as a position of power—something you achieve through hard work, intelligence, and perseverance. But as I grew in my leadership role, I began to realize that true leadership isn't about power or titles; it's about the mark you leave on others and the values you instill in them. That's your legacy.

One of my most significant moments of clarity came when I left a company I had been with for years. On my last day, as I reflected on my time there, I realized that my true contributions weren't the projects I had completed or the revenue I had generated. Instead, it was the people I had mentored, the culture I had helped build, and the sense of purpose I had instilled in my team. Those were the things that would continue to influence the company long after I was gone.

Your legacy isn't something you think about only when you're nearing the end of your career. It's something you shape every day, through every interaction and decision. It's about the people you lift up, the values you live by, and the changes you inspire in others.

8.1.2 The Ripple Effect of Leadership

One of the most profound lessons I've learned about leadership is that its effects ripple far beyond what we can see in the moment. A decision you make today can impact someone years down the line in ways you may never know.

I once mentored a young employee who was struggling to find her place in the company. She was bright, motivated, and hardworking, but she often doubted her abilities and was hesitant to take on leadership roles. I made it my mission to help her see her potential. I gave her opportunities to lead small projects, provided constructive feedback, and encouraged her to push past her comfort zone. Over time, I watched her grow into a confident and capable leader.

Years later, after I had moved on to a new role, I received an email from her. She had been promoted to a senior leadership position, and she told me that the confidence and skills she developed under my mentorship had been instrumental in her success. That moment was a powerful reminder of the ripple effect of leadership. The time and energy you invest in others can have a profound impact that continues long after you've left the picture.

8.1.3 How to Begin Building Your Legacy Now

Building a legacy doesn't happen overnight. It requires intentionality, self-reflection, and consistent action. One of the key steps I've taken to build my leadership legacy is to define my core values and live by them every day.

I once worked with a leader who, despite his incredible intelligence and strategic thinking, struggled to inspire loyalty in his team. The reason? His actions often contradicted his words. He would preach the importance of transparency and collaboration, but behind closed doors, he made decisions without consulting his team and withheld critical information.

That experience taught me a valuable lesson: if you want to leave a positive legacy, you must lead with integrity. Your actions need to align with your values, and you must consistently demonstrate the behaviors you want to inspire in others. The legacy you leave is built on the small, everyday choices you make—not just the big decisions.

One practical way to start building your legacy today is to think about how you can serve and empower others. Ask yourself, "How can I help the people around me grow and succeed? What values do I want to pass on to my team?" By focusing on these questions, you'll begin to shape a leadership legacy that will outlast your tenure.

8.2 Empowering Others to Lead

8.2.1 Multiplying Your Impact Through Others

If there's one thing I've learned in leadership, it's that your influence doesn't stop with you. As a leader, your greatest impact comes from empowering others to lead. By mentoring, coaching, and developing future leaders, you multiply your influence and create a legacy that extends far beyond your own direct actions.

There was a time when I was managing a large, high-performing team, and I realized that I couldn't be everywhere at once. I needed to empower my team members to take on leadership roles and make decisions independently. So, I started delegating more responsibility, giving them the tools and guidance they needed, but also the autonomy to make their own choices.

What I saw was incredible. My team not only rose to the occasion, but they also started to lead each other, collaborate more effectively, and innovate in ways I hadn't anticipated. My role shifted from being the central decision-maker to being a coach and mentor, helping them grow into leaders themselves. That experience reinforced my belief that true leadership is about multiplying your impact through others.

8.2.2 Building a Leadership Pipeline

One of the most rewarding aspects of leadership is watching the people you've mentored and developed step into leadership roles themselves. But this doesn't happen by accident—it requires intentional effort to build a leadership pipeline within your organization.

I've always believed in creating opportunities for leadership growth at all levels. In one organization, I implemented a formal leadership development program that identified high-potential employees early on and provided them with the resources, training, and mentorship they needed to grow. We created a structured path for leadership progression, with clear milestones and opportunities for hands-on leadership experience.

The result was a steady stream of emerging leaders who were prepared to step into larger roles as the organization grew. This not only ensured the company's long-term success but also created a culture where leadership development was embedded in the DNA of the organization. By building a leadership pipeline, you create a lasting impact that continues long after you've moved on.

8.2.3 Leaving a Lasting Organizational Impact

I once worked with a leader who, after years of service, retired from the company he helped build. But what struck me wasn't just the accolades he received during his farewell speech—it was the lasting impact he had on the organization's culture. His commitment to ethical decision-making, his emphasis on teamwork and collaboration, and his dedication to continuous improvement had become ingrained in the company's way of doing things. His legacy lived on through the values and systems he had instilled.

That experience reinforced for me that the most powerful legacy you can leave isn't just about personal success—it's about creating a culture and organizational structure that continues to thrive in your absence. Whether it's through implementing systems for continuous leadership development, fostering a culture of innovation, or ensuring that your values are reflected in the organization's long-term vision, the legacy you leave behind can shape the future of the organization for years to come.

8.3 Reflecting on Your Leadership Journey

8.3.1 Celebrating Wins and Learning from Losses

One of the most important aspects of leaving a lasting legacy is taking the time to reflect on your leadership journey. I've found that it's essential to celebrate your wins, both big and small, and to learn from your losses.

I'll never forget a particularly challenging project I led early in my career that ultimately failed. At the time, I was devastated—I had invested so much energy and passion into making it work. But looking back, I realize that the lessons I learned from that failure were invaluable. I gained a deeper understanding of my strengths and weaknesses as a leader, and I developed new strategies for managing complex projects. That failure, in many ways, shaped the leader I became.

As you reflect on your journey, take time to celebrate your successes, but don't shy away from acknowledging your failures. Both are integral to your growth as a leader and to the legacy you leave behind.

8.3.2 Looking Forward: What's Next?

As you reflect on your leadership legacy, it's also important to look forward. What's next in your leadership journey? What new challenges will you take on, and how will you continue to grow and evolve as a leader?

For me, this question came up when I transitioned out of a leadership role I had held for years. I wasn't sure what was next, but I knew I wanted to continue making an impact. That's when I decided to focus on mentoring the next generation of leaders, sharing the lessons I had learned, and helping others navigate their own leadership journeys.

Your leadership legacy isn't just about the past—it's about what comes next. As you continue to grow and evolve, your legacy will continue to take shape, inspiring others and creating lasting change long after you've moved on.

Leaving a lasting legacy as a leader is about more than just personal achievements. It's about empowering others, creating systems for long-term success, and living your values every day. Your leadership journey is ongoing, and the choices you make today will shape the legacy you leave behind. Start building that legacy now by focusing on how you can serve others, develop future leaders, and create a lasting impact that will continue long after you're gone.

www.ingramcontent.com/pod-product-compliance
Lightning Source LLC
Chambersburg PA
CBHW070151230526
45471CB00002B/608